Warm and Cold

Warm and Cold

David Mamet
and
Donald Sultan

GROVE PRESS
New York

Published by Grove Press
a division of Wheatland Corporation
920 Broadway
New York, N.Y. 10010

Library of Congress Cataloging-in-Publication Data

Mamet, David.
    Warm and cold/by David Mamet and Donald
Sultan.—1st ed.
        p.   cm.
    Summary: A poetic depiction of what keeps you warm
when it is cold, from good clothes and steam to the sound
of talk and the love that you keep with you wherever
you go.
    ISBN 0-8021-1084-3
    [1. American poetry.] I. Sultan, Donald, ill. II. Title.
PS3563.A4345W27   1988
811´.54—dc19   88-16311
                                                                        CIP
                                                                        AC

Manufactured in the United States of America
First Edition 1988
10 9 8 7 6 5 4 3 2 1

For Frances and Willa

**It's good to have good clothes on
in which you feel powerful
To be warm when you're cold**

To wear something that someone made for you

If you are far away from home

A keepsake will remind you of those who love you

You are on a train

Travelling away from them

but they are thinking of you

**Through the window you can see a man
going to work
"Inside his house" you think
"there is his family."
In smoke rising you see how cold it is**

**When you get off the train
they will say how cold it had
been last week or yesterday**

**And I want to sit in the café
It's warm there and the people
speak to one another earnestly**

The woolens smell of steam

A man can keep a picture
in his heavy shirt
You see in his face how well
he remembers what they all
did on that day

He holds the photograph

He puts the photograph away